Curls
and
Souls

JAID JONES

13TH & JOAN

For permission requests, write to the publisher, addressed "Attention: Permissions Coordinator," 205 N. Michigan Avenue, Suite #810, Chicago, IL 60601. 13th & Joan books may be purchased for educational, business or sales promotional use. For information, please email the Sales Department at sales@13thandjoan.com.

Printed in the U. S. A.

First Printing, September 2025

Library of Congress Cataloging-in-Publication Data has been applied for.

Paperback ISBN: 978-1-961863-98-9
Hardcover ISBN: 978-1-961863-86-6
Ebook ISBN: 978-1-961863-72-9

On April 19, 2024, my significant other and I
were told, "Trust Him."

I just want to thank Him for giving me a dream in
2014. It has taken 10 years for this dream to come
to fruition, but He made sure I saw it come true.

I also want to thank Him for creating my support
system that includes my significant other, family,
and closest friends. He blessed me with the people
meant to take this journey with me.

Jeremiah 29:11

"Getting our natural hair done can be one of the most frustrating processes in our daily routines. However, it is the style, the work of art at the end that makes the process worthwhile."

Service Menu

Preface

AS YOU BEGIN reading this book, my hope is that you trust the process. Just as when you get your hair done, there are times you get frustrated. There are times that you just want to stop the process and cut all of your hair off.

As you are reading this book, there may be some things that invoke a range of emotions. At times, you may be brought to tears or lost in deep thought. The words may jump off of the pages and feel like a heavy weight. Then, there are other times where you laugh, smirk, and smile.

I urge you to continue to push through and keep reading. At the end, just like your hair, you will have created something so beautiful, something that you are proud of and something that will be a direct reflection of the beauty inside of you.

Introduction

I REMEMBER when I first started writing this book. It began as a collection of quotes that I called "Poetic Vibez." Over time, I realized that I normally would have a surge in writing while I was having challenges in my relationships or once my relationships ended. I was trying to find a way to make sense of my pain. I started writing this manuscript in 2014. And for 10 years it sat as a Word document on my computer.

I finally realized that the reason it took so long to release the book was fear. I was afraid to expose my pain to the world and worried about being judged for my mistakes, especially those related to relationships. In that moment, I faced a decision. I could continue to delay the release of my book for another 10 years, or I could just put my fears to the side and finish what I started. When I finally finished the manuscript, it was more than freeing, I felt like I was able to bare my soul. It was healing on my own terms and on my own timing.

After I finished the manuscript, I realized I had not titled the book. I was at work one day going back and forth with different names when I started thinking about my natural hair journey. My hair and I had a love-hate relationship for years. I remember getting relaxers, braids, weaves, dyed my hair, and other protective styles. It wasn't until I started my natural hair journey back in 2013 that I realized how much damage I was doing to my hair. I had to learn how to take care of and fall in love with my hair. That process took years. I went from feeling like a silk press was the true definition of beauty to learning that my curls were just as beautiful. That's when I came up with the title: "Curls and Souls". Each section of the book represents different parts of the natural hair journey in alignment with the different stages of a relationship. Just like my romantic relationships were raw, beautiful, and could be painful, my relationship with my hair could be the same way. Both journeys represented more than just physical transformations. They represented the inner workings and transforming of my soul. Although at times both journeys were difficult, they led to transformations that were nothing short of beautiful. Out of my pain came beautiful beginnings.

"When I looked in the mirror, it was love at first curl."

Anonymous

Shampoo

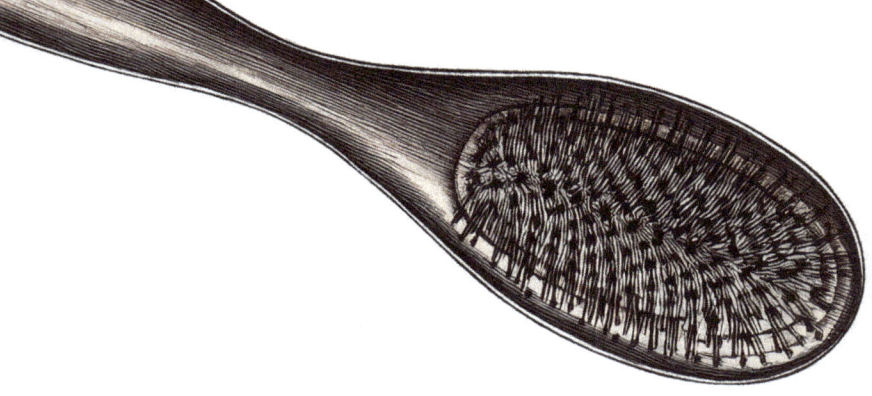

Serenity

Her laugh was contagious
Her smile could warm the coldest of hearts
Her hug was where you could feel safe
You found comfort in her

Beautiful Uproar

Deep down she scares you
You know your life would never be the same
She would be your beautiful storm
She would awaken something in you that would make
you think about being a better man
Maybe you aren't ready for that
Because deep down you know if you messed up and took
her for granted she would never be yours again

Eyes of the Storm

When she looked in his eyes she saw how the hues danced
with the sunlight
She proceeded to look deeper
And she glimpsed droplets of pain
They were like drops of rain
And with everything in her she wanted to wipe them away

Pretending

So we will sit there and gaze into each other's eyes and act
like it's nothing
I stop myself from reaching out to you
Stop one another from engaging in this dance
Because when I put my hand in yours
We both will not want to let go
So I'll stop and I'll pretend it's nothing
When it really is something
I have to accept that right now it can only be nothing
But I really wish it could be something

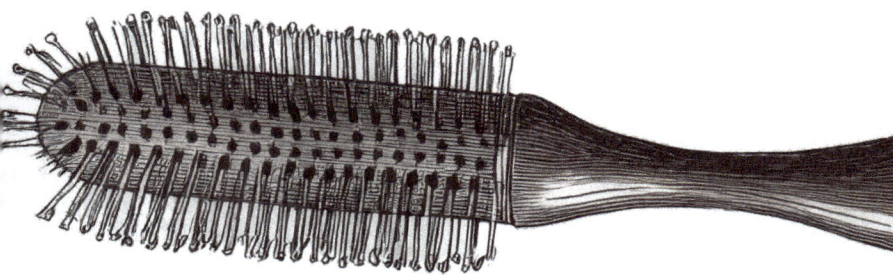

Second Thoughts

I wasn't supposed to feel with you
I wasn't supposed to love you
But I did
And there is always the chance of waking up one morning
Only for you to say you no longer love me
That this is something you don't want anymore
Saying that would hurt the most
Something like that could break me
It would catch my breath in my chest

Crossing Paths

He walked into her life
She walked into his
And from that day forward
Their lives were never the same

Empty Yearning

I wish I was your easiest hello and your hardest goodbye
I wish I knew if I captivated you with my presence and
left you breathless whenever I left
I wish I knew if you felt empty when I wasn't around

S.O.S

In that moment I felt like you needed me just as much
as I needed you
Because we weren't looking to save one another
We were seeking much more than that
In a world where we felt misunderstood
With you I saw someone who understood
In one another we saw pain that we hid from the world
We saw pain but we understood

Hold Me

As we are standing face-to-face
You pull me close to you
You rest your head against mine
And as both of us close our eyes we feel one another's pain
In that moment as we inhale and come closer
We hope that through this embrace the pain slips away

Uncomplicated

It was easy they said
It was easy to fall in love with her

Burning Twin Flames

When you spoke to me and touched me
I felt like you were touching my soul
I felt everything so deeply

Resting Cape

He wondered when was the last time someone took care
of her
She was always taking care of everyone else
She was always picking up the broken pieces
She was always willing to put smiles on the faces of
others
He saw the light in her amongst her hidden darkness
He wanted to take care of her
He wanted her to know what it was like to be at peace

Photograph

Time stopped
It was just a moment
But it was our moment
Let me stay in that moment with you
Let me take a snapshot
Because in that moment I was so happy
And I don't want that moment to fade away

Pause... Fast forward

That moment
I felt like it was real
To me it counted
To me it meant something
Timing
Maybe in another time
Maybe in another place
It could be everything we thought it could be

Loving Fortress

I wish you could wrap me in your arms and hold me
Because every time you do
My worries seem to fade away
I get the sense that you genuinely care about me
Or when you draw me closer and place a gentle kiss on my
forehead
I wish I could stay there with you forever just that way

At Ease

Unlike anyone else she was able to stop the rage and the pain
With her, your soul was at rest

Vibrational Equivalent

I would give anything to take your pain away
I would give anything for you to not feel so broken
The thing is that I understand how you feel
Because once upon a time that pain was mine

Sensation

And he drew her
Every line was perfection
Every curve was perfectly imperfect
Because through his hands he molded her
She allowed herself to be shaped by him
And after he finished the masterpiece
He had captured the true essence of her
He was looking at the definition of true beauty through
his own eyes

Stripped

Can he undress your mind?
Can he stimulate your soul?
Can he connect with you in every way without touching
you?

All Encompassing

I don't want to be your everything
I can't be your everything
Because reality sets in and if we both make each other
our everything
Then if one of us hurts the other one
When and if ever one of us walks away
You take everything with you
And I'm left with nothing

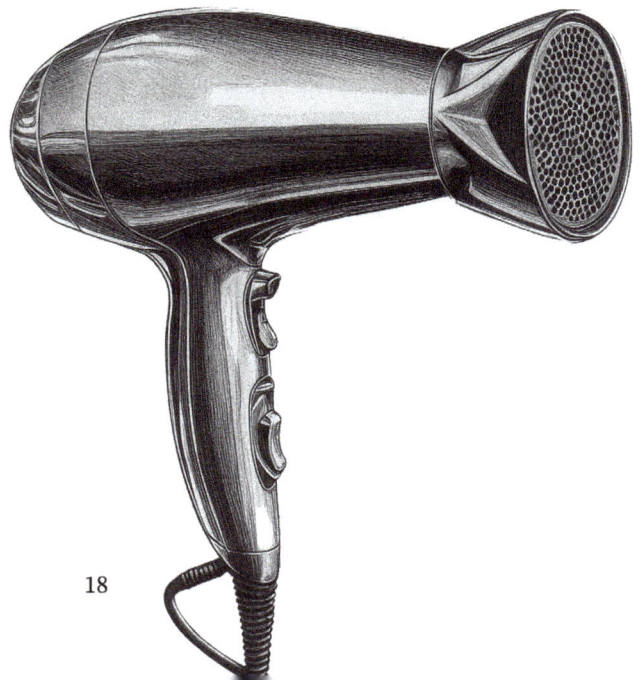

Candid Photographs

With you I feel like time does not matter
With you time stops
Being vulnerable with you has never been more scary
Yet it's also never been more beautiful
For once I really feel as if you don't want to change me
You see past the mask I put on for the rest of the world
Behind the smile you see that I have been hurt before
When you look at me I feel like you can see through me
You can see the pain in my eyes
And the more time I spend with you
I see that you will do even the smallest of things to make
sure that for a while
I forget about that pain

Shadow

I stood beside him
Didn't walk in front or behind him
Crawled with him
Fell down with him
Prayed with him
I tried to be the reason he got back up again

Contemplation

If I decided to leave one day
Would you stop me?
What if I decided that I wasn't strong enough to do this?
Keep us together
Would you stop me?
Am I worth waiting for?
See I treasure the moments that we share
From the unexpected kisses
To the hugs that I wish would linger
Because if I could stay in your arms forever I would
So, if I decided to leave one day would you stop me?
Would your heart stop?
Would you reach out for me?
Grab my arm and slowly turn me around?
Hold my face in your hands?
Look into my eyes and figure out the reason I am doing
this?
And realize that I could potentially be the one that got
away
Can't you see that I'm the only one that hasn't left?
The one that would give my everything to never see you
fall
Never want to see you hurting
Because if you were hurting, I would be there to take the
pain away and make it mine
That's love
So, if I decided to leave one day
Would you stop me?
Would you be able to breathe?

Would you miss me as much?
See I could smile
And yet would you take the time to see the silent tears
that I cry?
So, if I decided to leave would you stop me?
Would you recognize that empty space?
Would you sit there and act like you weren't hurting?
Would you reach out for me?
Would you be strong enough?
Wonder what I'm thinking?
Wonder where I am in relation to where you are?
Tell me that you need me as much as I need you
Tell me that you want me in your life
Just in case I decided to leave one day
I would hope that you would stop me
Show me that I'm the person you want and need
Because I don't want to be the one that got away

My Love Letter to Love

Dear Love,

I sit here and reflect on your presence in my life. Sometimes I call out to you, but you don't respond, and nothing can fill the void of your absence. You can be perplexing and, at times, one of the most challenging people I've ever encountered. You can hurt me like no other. Then you expect me to pick up the pieces of my broken heart, and put the pieces back together myself when you are the reason my heart broke in the first place. Sometimes I hate the way you make me feel. You make me feel like I'm always wrong and that it's my fault when things don't go right. I make sacrifices and pour my heart out to you, but you don't realize everything within the fully painted picture. You sit back as I cry tears of agony and suffering. The tears fall from my eyes creating puddles of pain, depression, and loneliness around my feet. The pain you cause is enough to stop my breath, cause my heart to skip a beat and leave a hole in my chest. It's an empty feeling, something that makes you feel surreal. Love, why do you hurt me the way that you do? How can you be so much of a rollercoaster and think that I am supposed to stay along for the tumultuous ride? How can you be the reason I smile one minute, and the reason why I cry the next? Why do you make me pay for your mistakes? Why do you condemn me and tear me down when you are supposed to build me up? You promised that you would always be there for me, yet you walk in and out of my

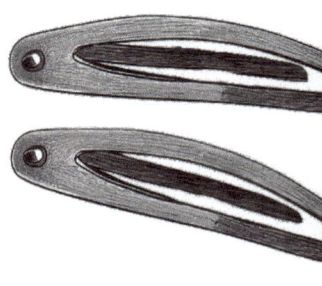

life expecting me to be the same way I was before you left me. God says you never fail, but sometimes I hurt so badly because I feel like you fail me. I want to believe in you. I want to believe that you are real. But most of all I want to know that you are the best thing that can happen to me. I want to believe in you. I want to have faith in you. So, if I'm investing this much in you, just think of me the next time you decide to hurt me because I don't know if I can go through that again. Love me the way that I love you.

Sincerely,

A Wounded Heart

My Love Letter to Love Part II

Dear Love,

A while ago I wrote to you, trying to understand why I had you in my life. I tried to figure out why every time I was hurt, you failed to realize that you played some part in the reason why I was hurting. As these couple of weeks have gone by, I am beginning to realize that you have to go away in order for people to realize why you were there in the first place. Death should not have to come knocking at the door for people to realize that you always survive. I don't want to turn my back on you knowing that you are so amazing, and that you could potentially change my life. I don't want to go to sleep mad, knowing that if I didn't wake up the next morning that I didn't get a chance to tell you how much you meant to me. The fights and the arguments are not important because they only create a hazy mist that brings about confusion, pain, and heartache. You can stand the test of time, yet people act as if they have all of the time in the world forgetting that tomorrow is not promised to anyone. I just want you to know that I trust you until you give me a reason not to, that I'm here for you unless you treat me in a way that I do not deserve. I just want you to realize that I am stronger than what you may think at times. If someone cares about you enough to love you despite your imperfections, if they may not understand every aspect of who you are but are patient enough to climb over every wall you put up, just to get a little closer and prove that nothing can stand in the way

of truly loving you—then you've found something rare and profound. Both you and I make mistakes, and both you and I know that just because you don't love me the way I want you to, that doesn't mean that you don't love me. I just want us to limit the hurtful words, limit the fights, limit the thunder that can shake our household creating thunderstorms of fallen teardrops because if we didn't wake up tomorrow, I would want to cherish a happy memory. I would want to remember that feeling of security and that place of peacefulness when you say, "I love you."

Sincerely,

A Heart that's Healing

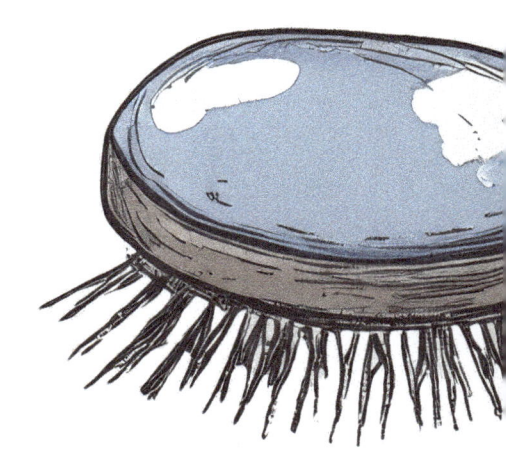

Overpass

I want
I feel
I want to ignore it
I want to make it seem like it doesn't exist
Because in each moment, time stops
I find it hard to catch my breath
I forget to breathe
Breathe in
Breathe out
That's what I tell myself
When I'm around you the energy is different
I find myself asking what is it?
But I get no answer
I have to calculate each and every move
Because I can't lose control with you
Let the fire burn out
Let the desire not be there
But no matter how hard I try
I can't act like it's nothing
Maybe it is something

Pearl

Can he touch your soul without touching you physically?

Fairy Tale

Once upon a time she was the girl you always wanted

Stand in the Gap

Love me when I'm not strong enough to love myself

Conditioner

Boxing Gloves

Give me a reason
Give me a reason to fight
Give me a reason to stay in the ring with you
Give me a reason to stop myself from walking to the
door, turning the knob, and walking out
Stop me from making a decision where I never come
back
Give me a reason to forgive one more time
Because all I want is a reason

Unwritten Poison

He said he would always be there for me
It was like poison rolling off his tongue
His words would be the death of me

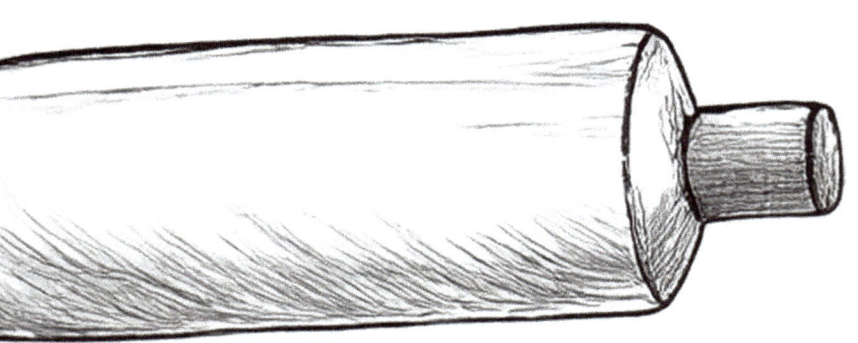

Flatline

You said you couldn't breathe without her
But when she left is when you took your last breath

Questions

Why wouldn't you want the girl every guy wanted?
Why would you let her slip out of your grasp when all
she wants is you?
Why wouldn't you appreciate the fact that her loyalty
lies with you and only you?
Why wouldn't you step back and say,
"Damn, out of everyone she could have been with, she
chose me."
You won't ask yourself these questions
Because you don't want to face the fact that she is
everything you could have ever wanted

Emotional Incarceration

I'm leaving **myself in this mental** prison when it comes
to you
There's no way out but I can't stay in
Because with you the road is leading to the unknown
I feel stuck
You don't want me, but you can't live without me
You don't want me
But you don't want anyone else to have me
I need to know if you need me
Because I can't need you
But if I knew you needed me as much as I thought you did
I could let go and realize I needed you too
Because by wanting and needing you in my life
I'm vulnerable and that leaves me in a place not protected
Because I need to protect myself even from you
Experience has been my greatest teacher
She has left me with more questions than answers
I can't be naïve with you
I was no longer jaded a long time ago

I need you to need me because I can't handle needing
you when you don't feel the same
But I need to get off this rollercoaster ride
Because it is taking me to a destination I don't know
where I could end
Because I just want to know if I'm going to end up alone
I need to know that you won't be there
Let me prepare
Because then I can prepare for the hurt
It won't weigh on me like a ton of bricks
Because I can't be locked away in your mental prison
I can't fall under your gravity
Not if you don't feel the same...

Shelter

You told me,
"Don't be scared of me.
This isn't right.
This isn't how it is supposed to be.
I will protect you from anyone or anything that tries to
hurt you."
And I said,
"What if the thing or person I need protection from is you?"

We're No Longer

I don't know what hurts more
Hearing someone say they no longer can love you
Or looking them straight in the eyes as they tell you it will
never be you

Flirting With Perjury

Sealed with a kiss
Lies upon lips
The sweetest words
Let the truth unfold

Distant Voyeur

She was yours
You didn't appreciate her
Now you watch from a distance
As someone else loves and appreciates the girl you took
for granted

Pretty Porcelain

He was a collector of dolls
She was a glass baby doll
He held her and then let her go
He didn't reach out to catch her
As she hit the ground, she broke
Shards of glass were strewn all over the floor
And that's where he left her
Broken

Taking the Easy Way Out

For him it was easier to just push her away
Rather than look her in the eyes and tell her that he
could not be with her
He could not bear seeing the consequence of a
heartbreak right in front of him

Poser

When he turned out to be everything he said he wasn't
I knew I would have to let him go

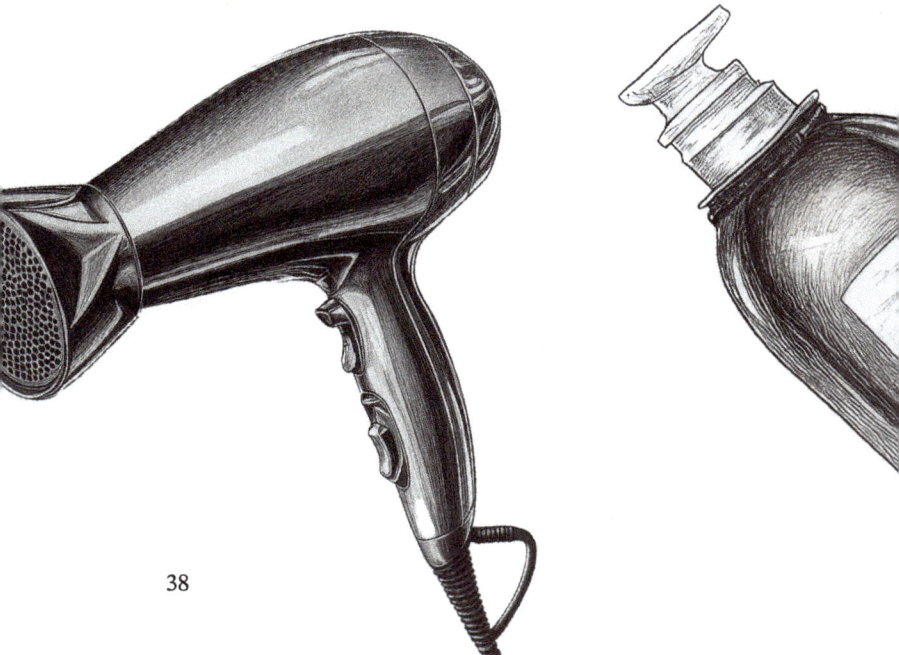

His Fragility

Because of how weak he was
He couldn't see the strength in her
He didn't know how to love her

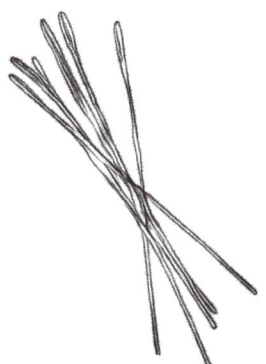

Short—lived vs. Forever

Having to let someone that you care about go is a
temporary pain
But I'd rather have temporary pain than everlasting
heartache

In Conclusion.

Unfortunately, our bond had an expiration date
Our time together is no more

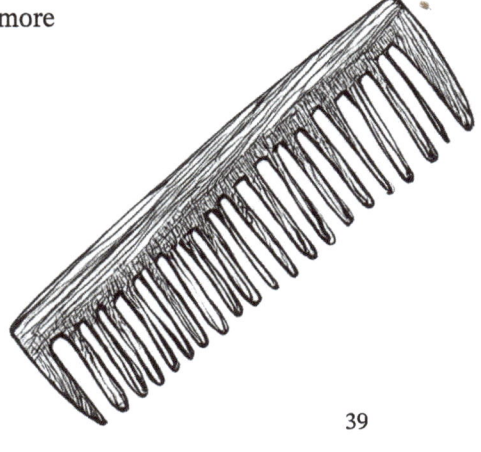

Unlocked

I opened the door
I let you in
I wish I hadn't
Because now you have the key
The key to the place I wouldn't let anyone else in
Because by opening the door
You opened the door to my soul

Withdrawals

I didn't mean as much
You sold dreams that turned into nightmares
Hopes that turned into hopelessness
And a balance that was negative in the account of what I
thought was our love
No longer do I believe in you
A wolf in sheep's clothing
I should have believed your words
You didn't protect me
You tried to salvage what was left of yourself
I knew there was a reason
I just did not know the reason
Thank you for painting me another reality
You're the reason why I am jaded

Fairy Knots

Let me untangle myself from the web I have woven
Let me fall from underneath your gravity
Let me push rewind and delete on every memory
Allow myself to escape from every should have
Could have
Or would have
Because now it's, "But, I didn't."
Let me place you in the figurative box and leave you
there
You won't need to come out of it
You won't need to do anything but stay inside
That way I can just meet you there
And I will have relinquished you of any worry or
concern that came with anything that was outside the
box I painted for you
Let the lines be drawn in the sand
Let's not cross those lines
Because for now I must settle

Dead Harvest

Let your words match your actions
Don't awaken something in her if you didn't plan on
watching her bloom
You watered the flower and then you pulled out her
roots
Then you tried to replant her as if you were waiting for
her to bloom
But once you pulled at her roots
You should have known she would never be the same
flower again

Smashed to Pieces

When you love someone, you don't break them just
because you're broken too

Her Stillness

You know you truly hurt her when she is silent
You know you hurt her when she has nothing left to say
to you

Fixation

You were my high
And it was an addiction
It was a dangerous addiction
Because once I came down
Once I was done with getting my fix of you
I was empty
I was empty and alone

Morning Fog

I don't know what hurts more
The fact that I gave you my all and it still meant nothing
Or the fact that I lost myself trying so hard to hold onto you
You were the air that I breathed
Many of my waking moments were consumed of trying to make you happy
Trying to figure out what I needed to stop doing wrong
So that you would love me the way you loved me at the beginning
But you didn't love me
I don't know if you ever did

Unsealed Envelopes

Sometimes in my moments of silence
When I'm by myself
My mind takes me back to all the memories that were wrapped around me and you
And then my mind races forward to the last words you said to me
Your words were ugly
They replay in my mind like a record player
You said you would be an amazing partner to someone else
But that it would never be me
That was all you needed to say

Hangover

One of the worst feelings in the world is waking up one morning
And the person you love telling you that they don't love you anymore

Adornment

I wore loyalty like a necklace
It was beautiful
It adorned the essence of a part of me
But you turned my loyalty into a noose around my neck
And before I knew it you hung me with it
Led to the death of me

Preferences

I had to come to the realization that it won't be me
You will never choose me

Silent Loathing

There is nothing worse in the world than hating the
person you love
It is nothing like sitting there with the pain of knowing
the person you thought you knew is not that person
anymore
And realizing the image of who you thought that person
was is tarnished
You will never picture them the same way again

Unspoken Truths

I don't know what hurts more
The person saying that they don't love you or want to be
with you anymore
Or the person making you feel that you are the loneliest
person in the world
And you knowing deep in your heart that person does
not want to be with you
Yet will never give you enough respect to come out and
say it

HER

You said there was something about her
That you didn't love her but that you had a connection
with her
You said that you just needed some time to figure out
who you wanted to be with
She said that you would pick me
But I said you would pick her
Again, you said that you just needed time
And then I told you that I was going to make a decision
for you
I told you that you were going to pick her because if you
had really loved me, there would be no her

Damaged Flowers

I bleed
I remember the blood as it rolled down my face
When the skin of your fist met the skin of my cheek
How in that moment beauty became acquainted with
the beast
That moment changed everything
I knew that I had fallen in love with my enemy because
there is no way that my true love could permanently scar
me
There is no way that my true love could give me a daily
reminder of such an ugly truth
I didn't belong there
I knew I should have left one too many times before
But somehow, I convinced myself if I could almost stick
to the directions, then maybe I could get it right
I hurt myself the more I tried to love you because at
the end of the day my love couldn't fix how broken of a
person you were
And as a result, I became broken in the process
I spent so much time trying to prove my love to you
Gave so much of myself to the relationship that by the
end
I had no love for myself
I was empty
A walking corpse
Because physically I was breathing
But internally I had already died inside
Me being a good woman was never going to be good
enough
I could lie and say that once things ended for good that I
was okay

But that would be another ugly truth
Because at times I still have nightmares
I wake up at night sometimes holding myself as if I'm
trying to protect myself from your touch
How sometimes in the most random times I hear your
voice in the back of my head
And I cringe
Because the voice spits venom of destructive opinions of
who you thought I was
I was your trophy but for some reason to you
And a reason unknown to me I was never good enough
to love
Even now as years have passed, I just want to be out of
reach of your gravity
To be rid of the paralyzing fear that no one could love
me
Or that someone could hurt me like you did
I want to be normal
I want to be okay
I don't want what happened to me to make me so
damaged that I am damaged beyond repair
Because that wouldn't be fair
That wouldn't be fair to love
To life
And it wouldn't be fair to my need to be free from the
chains of my past
A past that sometimes I feel like just won't set me free

On a Loop

I'm wondering if coming second was a blessing or a
curse
She didn't love enough, and I wonder if I loved too much
Never knew how hard it would be to love someone who
had been hurt before
More than once, I wanted to leave
But I stopped myself before reaching the door
Turning the knob right or left meant either turning time
forward or back
Forward to the unknown of what we could or couldn't be
Back to a time when hurt was all we knew
And I can't lie
We have our good times
When I fall asleep in your arms as the moon looks down
upon us
And when we wake up in the morning the sun peaks
through the window and smiles at us
When laughing outweighs the tears I cry
The loneliness you feel or the feelings you hide
But when we fight, instead of shutting out the world we
shut out each other
We spit venom, poison creeping into our veins as it
travels to our hearts
We try so hard to forget not wanting to remember what
it was like
What it was like to hurt one another in those heated
moments of anger
Before we know it, the damage is done
The words are etched in our memories

That's when looking in each other's eyes and saying,
"I'm sorry" is what it comes to
How many times can we rewrite a written story?
How many times can we say I'm sorry?
Time is running out
The race is coming to an end
Either it works and we cross the finish line together
Or it doesn't, and we cross alone

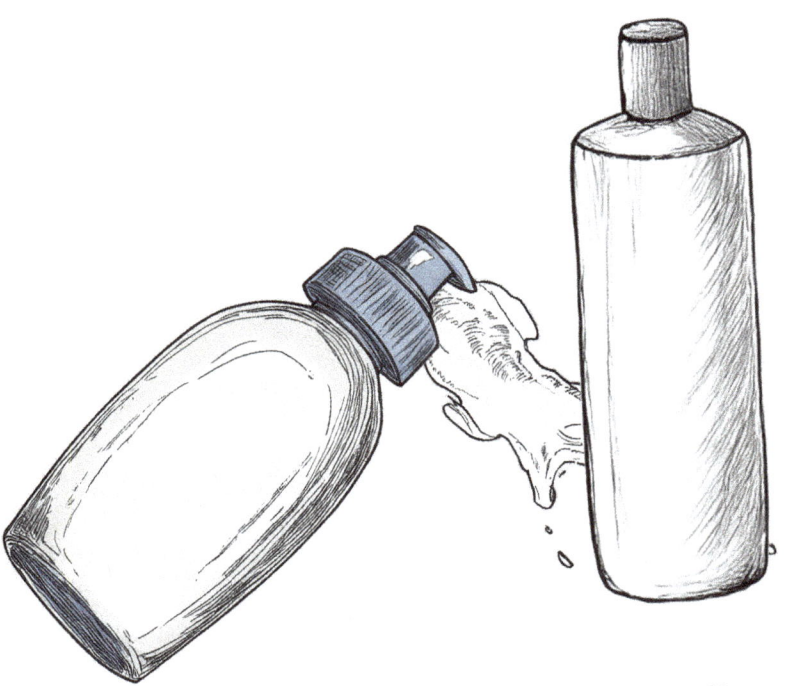

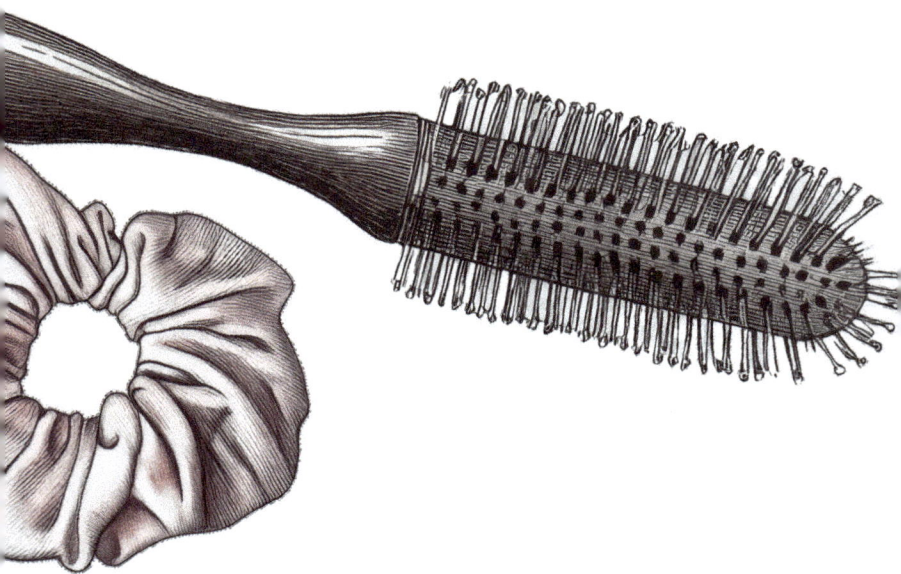

"Now I Lay Me Down to Sleep..."

I listened to every lie as the lies wove themselves into a
blanket
A blanket of betrayal and deception
A blanket you brought into our home
And then you thought by covering me, you were doing
me a favor

Superwoman's Cape

I tried to be strong for you
Even when you continued to string me along
Yet I continued to love you anyways
And was still there for you after you said, "I lost myself"
or "I needed space..."

Cross Country

I still managed to walk miles in my heels
in the midst of my tears
Even when I carried your burdens on top of my own

Eau De Toilette

You didn't realize that I noticed the traces of her lipstick
I knew they weren't mine
I smelled the remnants of her perfume
I knew it was not mine
Because I wore Amor Amor
You were covered with my love
But to smell her perfume on you meant that you chose
something else to wear
There was nothing left of me on the traces of your skin

Relentless

I bent and broke my back
I found the strength to be strong for you
Even when I couldn't be strong for myself
I continued to push forward even when the scars you left
Hurt worse than when the wounds were first placed there

Aborted Mission

I had the courage to stay
But after a while I had to walk away
Because at the end of the day, I did everything I could for you
And you didn't appreciate me
You tried to strip me of who I was
You could never take responsibility for your actions
You continued to blame me for everything you caused
And you didn't care that it tore me apart

Parallelogram

I called you
You didn't answer
I put my hand out beside me
But you didn't put your hand in mine
I looked behind me, you weren't there
I looked in front of me
And you weren't there
I looked beside me
And you weren't there
And that's when I needed you the most

Fraternal

In that moment I was no longer your equal
Because you don't treat your equal that way
You don't talk to your equal that way
You don't come out and say you don't care about your equal
that way
You meant what you said because you were angry
Words dipped in venom
Straight shot
Can't block them out
In that moment I wasn't your equal
I was beneath you
Let me search between black and white because there is no
gray
You say you love me, but you hate me
You hate me because I remind you of everything you are not
I challenge you
And although you love me you hate me
Your hatred showed
I'm not your equal
You don't hurt your equal
I don't know what I am
But you don't treat me like your equal

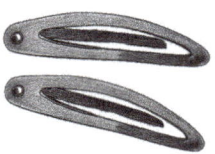

Demolition

You don't love her
Because you don't destroy people that you love

Abhorrence

I hate that I listened to you
I hate that I believed you when you said you loved me

Creed

We must have different definitions of what is and what
isn't
Yet these repetitive cycles have no ending
Marked by love
Scarred by a curse
In the midst of it all there is confusion
I don't know who's right or who's wrong
When will we ever know?

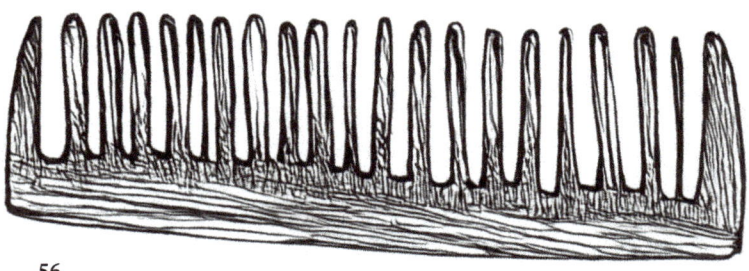

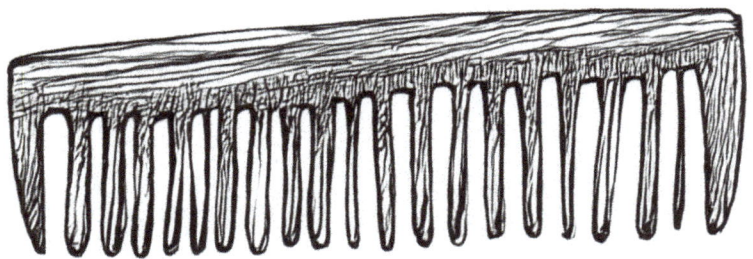

Blemish

A trace of a scar can bring back a hint of how ugly you
are
And how loving you was one of my biggest mistakes

Not for a Moment

You never loved her
You just wanted to stay connected to her
You never deserved her
And by letting her go she was finally set free

Incommunicative

Silence does more damage than actions could ever do

Time Travel

If only it was a **different time**
Place
Hour
Minute
Or second
Just maybe it could have been everything we hoped for
But life doesn't always work that way
And time for some reason is working against us
I wish it wasn't
I hope one day we could see if it could be something
But like I always say
Right now I have to accept that it's nothing
But I wish it could be something

Seashells and Seahorses

If I could count the drops of the ocean
They couldn't compare to the number of tears I have
shed over you ruining every part of me

Ancient Remains

And you relished in the beauty of ruining me

Bottom of the Abyss

How deep does the hurt go?

Laws of Motion

We love those that hurt us and hurt those that love us

Cupholders and Coasters

See you're the type of dude that made each girl feel
special
In each of their own moments
Your actions fleeting
She couldn't get too comfortable with you because she
was never secure with you
A placeholder
It was never real for you from the beginning

Last Curtain Call

I don't know what's worse
The fact that I deserved everything but didn't want for
anything
And yet you still couldn't show up

Message in a Bottle

Saying goodbye to you broke me more than it was ever
going to break you

Style

Soul Cries

And then her soul cried
It cried for who she loved
It cried for what she lost

Broken Mirrors

She could only be herself
She could only be real
Her imperfections
Her flaws
Her strengths
Her weaknesses
All wrapped into loving herself

Her Antidote

She craved being alone sometimes
She clung to it like a drug
She needed that fix
Because the danger in wanting to be alone is that she
had no problem resting there
She came out of the depths of being alone when she was
ready

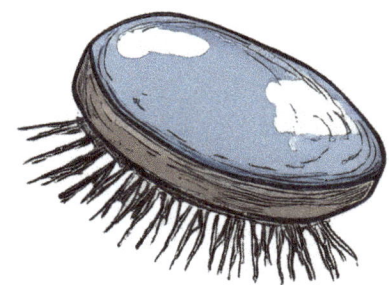

Anesthesia

And if I could not feel I wouldn't
If I could just be numb I would

Shattered

And then she broke
But she broke beautifully
Because in the midst of her brokenness
God gave her the strength to be whole again

Once More

Through her brokenness she still managed to love again
She still managed to try one more time

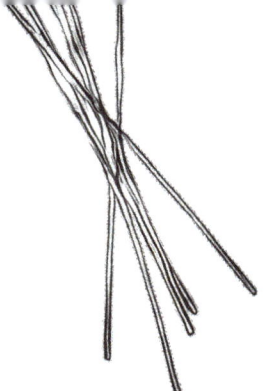

Unbound

I'm searching for home
A place where I am free from all chains
Where my heart and mind are out of bondage
Where my wings aren't clipped
Where I can feel free
Where I can fly so effortlessly

Unseen Agony

Her pretty smile hid the ugliest of pains

Invisible Shackles

She wasn't meant to be bound by chains
Those chains were things and people
She was supposed to be free
She was meant to be free

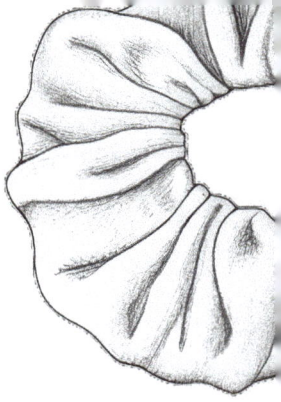

Void

I don't know what to feel
But I don't want to feel anything

Shortfalls

My worth was never defined by the lack of your ability
to love me
Your inability to love me was because you were unable
to love yourself

Reminisce

Those happy moments
She cherished them
She held them close
Because they were few and far in between
Those moments were like hourglasses
Once the sand ran out
The memory faded

Sincerity

She wanted something real
Authentic
Because her past was a reminder of the fact that even
though she had done right by others not everyone had
the same heart as she did
How they asked for something just as real
And when they had it
They treated the bond as if it meant nothing
Because you can't look her in her face and tell her that
you love her
And turn around and hurt her
The same way you praise her
You turn around and use words to bring her down
See she wanted something real
Like blood running through her veins
She wanted something real
She didn't want the connection to be real and then
become tainted
She would rather be alone
Because she would rather love herself
Than to have someone say they love her and treat her
less than extraordinary

Swimming to the Surface

There is nothing like feeling like you're drowning
But when you cut off whatever is sucking the life out of
you
How beautiful it is to be free
How beautiful it is to breathe again

Enclosure

They said she was difficult
That she had too many walls up
But if you knew what she had been through
You would understand why
Because once upon a time someone promised they
would never hurt her
It was the biggest lie she ever heard

When the City Sleeps

It was at night when everything hit her
Everything she didn't want to think about
Every fear
Every doubt that she tried to push away during the day
Those thoughts came out to play at night
Her thoughts danced with the streetlights
They robbed her of not only her sleep
But also of the peace that she desperately craved

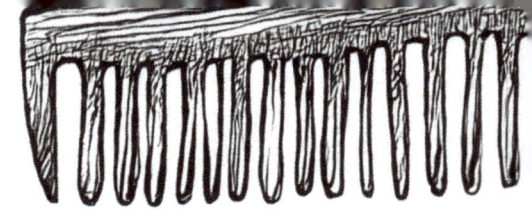

Temporary Remedy

It was the company she kept
Text messages
Phone calls
Dates
She used them to fill the void
They were Band-Aids for the pain she didn't want to
deal with

Immerse

She finds herself drowning
She's swimming just to reach the surface
She's reaching
Grabbing for anything to hold onto
Anything to keep her from letting the waves overtake her
and pull her further under
With anything she wants to reach the surface
So she can finally know what it's like to breathe again

Relay

She realized that first place was not going to happen
Settling for second place was not an option
She sought more than that
She deserved more than that
So rather than settle for less than she deserved
She excused herself from the race

Vindication

I will absolve you of everything
Every emotion
Every feeling
I will absolve you of everything when it comes to me

Laying Down Burdens

By realizing what was causing the weight, she was able
to set herself free

Overpass

Out of all the people in the world
One day someone will meet me on that bridge
That one person will make me realize why everyone else
that showed up and everyone else that came and didn't
stay won't even matter

Enchanted Dismay

When you stop to realize that there is beauty in every
disappointment
That is when moving on won't be so hard
That is when you can live and learn
When you can make beautiful mistakes and learn from
the most painful lessons
The most painful lessons being matters of the heart

Imprinted

It's that empty space
When I lay in bed at night where you used to lay
It's empty
It's cold
Because with everything I wish that you could wrap me
in your arms
And we talk until the sun rises
But when morning comes, and I open my eyes
I turn to my side and realize that this is my reality
I'm living life without you

Passports and Baccations

One day you will look back
You will look back and realize why nobody else that
failed to show up
Showed up late
Or showed up and left
They won't matter
One day someone will meet you on the bridge
Grab your hand
and say, 'I'm sorry I took so long. But I'm here now.
Now, that I got you, where are we going?"

Reality Check

Every once in a while I will get a text saying you miss me
How it makes no sense that you have to find out how I
am doing by looking at my Facebook
Or look at the most recent pictures on my Instagram
Then I have to remind you that we are where we are
because of you
We aren't together because of you
You tried to dim my light because you were unhappy
with your own light
The truth is no matter how much you say you miss me
I don't miss you
Because you gave me no choice but to figure out how to
live my life without you

Holding

She gave a new meaning to what it was like to fall in
love with a beautiful storm
She was always within his grasp but never completely
his
She was never completely anyone's
Because to love her was one thing
But to fall in love with her was something completely
different

Studying

I'm still learning to love Love
Once a upon a time when I loved Love
He didn't love me back

Consciousness

If breathing meant I had to take a breath without you
I would choose to live

Road Map to Nowhere

I'm searching for a place called home
Not really sure what or who home is

Forever Fleeting

I want to feel everything but at the same time feel
nothing at all

Carmen

Her beauty was her tragedy and that's why they thought
they could hurt her

Diablo's Lover

I created heaven out of my solitude of hell

Fire and Brimstone

I'm drowning in the abyss of going nowhere

Silent Headphone Party

Because of the pain you gave me, you have turned me into a wounded extrovert

Lovely Ascension

She just had a dope soul

Acknowledgements

I WOULD NOT BE where I am today without Him. Over the years I prayed and asked questions. Why am I here? What was my purpose? What was my calling? Through prayer and spending time with Him, He taught me that those questions don't always have easy answers and that we may not get the answers we expect. However, everything that occurred happened the way it was supposed to happen. Nothing is by happenstance. All those times I thought I was alone, He was right there walking beside me. When I was too weak to walk, He carried me.

"In the end, allow your curls to be the window to your soul."

About the Author

In 2025, **JAID JONES**, a Baltimore native, would go on to release her first poetry book, "Curls and Souls." Through a mixture of love, pain, and strength Jaid has bought a raw and rich perspective to the literary world. Jaid and one of her triplet siblings, began taking writing seriously while they were students at the University of Florida. While at the University of Florida, she was able to grow her love for writing and poetry through participating at events hosted by the auxiliary group, Poets Inc. Jaid and her sister were able to perform at several spoken word and poetry night events while completing their undergraduate degrees. Growing up, Jaid and her siblings loved to read and went to the library once a week to check out their favorite library books.